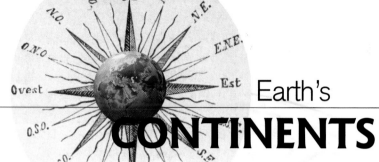

Earth's
CONTINENTS

Continents

Bruce McClish

www.heinemann.co.uk/library

Visit our website to find out more information about Heinemann Library books.

To order:

 Phone 44 (0) 1865 888066

Send a fax to 44 (0) 1865 314091

Visit the Heinemann Bookshop at www.heinemann.co.uk/library to browse our catalogue and order online.

First published 2003 in Austrailia by Heinemann Library a division of Harcourt Education Australia, 18–22 Salmon Street, Port Melbourne Victoria 3207 Australia (a division of Reed International Books Australia Pty Ltd, ABN 70 001 002 357).

© Reed International Books Australia Pty Ltd 2003
First published in paperback in 2005.
The moral right of the proprietor has been asserted.

Editor: Carmel Heron
Designer: Stella Vassiliou
Photo researcher: Margaret Maher
Production controller: Chris Roberts
Maps and diagrams by Pat Kermode and Stella Vassiliou

Film separations by Digital Imaging Group (DIG), Melbourne, Australia
Printed in China by WKT Company Ltd.

ISBN 1 74070 126 7 (hardback)
07 06 05 04 03
10 9 8 7 6 5 4 3 2 1

ISBN 0 431 18161 6 (paperback)
09 08 07 06 05
10 9 8 7 6 5 4 3 2 1

British Library Cataloguing in Publication Data
McClish, Bruce.
Earth's continents - (All About Continents)
910
A full catalogue record for this book is available from the British Library.

Acknowledgements
The author would like to thank: Avi Olshina, geologist, Victorian Government; Peter Nunan, geography teacher, Royal Geographical Society of Queensland; Craig Campbell, researcher; Jenny McClish, researcher and contributing author.

Main cover image of the Purnululu (Bungle Bungle) Range, Australia, supplied by Coo-ee Picture Library.

Other images supplied by: Auscape/Jean-Paul Ferrero: pp. 7, 17, /K. Schafer & Peter Arnold: p. 13, /S. Wilby & C. Ciantar: p. 12; ANT Photo Library/G. E. Schmida: p. 25; Coo-ee Picture Library: pp. 14, 19 (bottom), 21; Image Addict: p. 5; © The Natural History Museum (London): p. 8; PhotoDisc: pp. 15, 16, 18, 19 (top), 24, 27.

Every attempt has been made to trace and acknowledge copyright. Where an attempt has been unsuccessful, the publisher would be pleased to hear from the copyright owner so any omission or error can be rectified in subsequent printings.

Contents

What is a CONTINENT?

Continents are the largest bodies of land on Earth. We generally speak of seven continents: Europe, Asia, Africa, North America, South America, Australia and Antarctica. A continent is not really the same thing as a country, although one continent (Australia) is also a country. A continent is usually much larger than a country, and its boundaries are determined by natural features, such as seas and mountain ranges, rather than a border agreed upon by people.

Changing ideas

Ideas about the continents have changed over time. Fifty years ago, scientists believed that the continents were fixed, standing in the same place for billions of years. Today, we know that this idea is wrong. The continents are not standing still. Fossils give evidence that the continents moved thousands of kilometres during ancient times, and measurements show that they are still moving today.

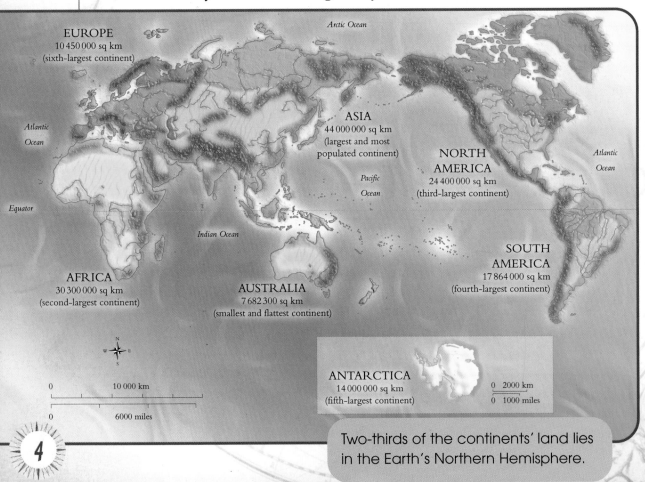

EUROPE
10 450 000 sq km
(sixth-largest continent)

Arctic Ocean

ASIA
44 000 000 sq km
(largest and most populated continent)

NORTH AMERICA
24 400 000 sq km
(third-largest continent)

Atlantic Ocean

Atlantic Ocean

Pacific Ocean

Equator

Indian Ocean

SOUTH AMERICA
17 864 000 sq km
(fourth-largest continent)

AFRICA
30 300 000 sq km
(second-largest continent)

AUSTRALIA
7 682 300 sq km
(smallest and flattest continent)

N
W · E
S

0   10 000 km

0   6000 miles

ANTARCTICA
14 000 000 sq km
(fifth-largest continent)

0   2000 km
0   1000 miles

Two-thirds of the continents' land lies in the Earth's Northern Hemisphere.

Atlantis was a legendary continent. It supposedly existed thousands of years ago, in the Atlantic Ocean. A Greek legend tells of an ancient civilisation that thrived on Atlantis, with great wealth, beautiful palaces and powerful rulers. But an Earth-shaking disaster struck the continent and it completely sank into the ocean, destroying the people and their civilisation. According to this legend, the people of Atlantis had become corrupt and greedy, and the destruction was a punishment from the gods.

Joining the continents

Even the way we speak about the continents has changed. For example, we know that Europe and Asia are not really separate continents. Europe and Asia are joined in a more massive continent we now call Eurasia. Some **geographers** believe that Africa is not a true continent, either. It is also joined with Eurasia, and the two continents together could be called Eurafrasia.

Although Eurasia or Eurafrasia may be more exact terms, most people still use the old names Europe, Asia and Africa when speaking of the continents. They do this because the names are so familiar, and people are accustomed to them when speaking about culture, travel and world events.

Continents and the Earth

The continents are more than great **landmasses**. They have an important effect on the Earth, living things and human history. The movement of continents causes Earth-shaping events, like the build-up of mountains or the widening of valleys. The position of continents affects weather, the shape of oceans and the pattern of their currents. The boundaries of continents often determine the natural range of different plants and animals – and even where people speak different languages and practise different customs.

Continents contain a wide variety of landscape features, including mountains and deserts.

The make-up of
CONTINENTS

The continents can be very different in size, shape, climates and cultures. Yet all continents have certain things in common. They all have very ancient rocks, including some that are billions of years old. They all have immense areas of land, from below sea level to thousands of metres above sea level (sea level is the level that is even with the surface of the sea). With so much land area, the continents contain a wide variety of landscape features – mountains, valleys, deserts, plains, rivers and lakes. Some islands lying nearby can also be considered part of a continent. For example, the British Isles are considered part of Europe, and Greenland is considered part of North America.

Continents and the Earth's crust

All continents are part of the Earth's crust. This is the outermost layer of rocks that covers the Earth. Below the crust are deeper, thicker layers known as the **mantle** and the **core**. These deep layers of the Earth are very hot, and contain large amounts of **molten rock**. The crust has two parts: the continents (or continental crust) and the ocean floor (or oceanic crust). The continents are the bulkiest part of the crust, around 20–70 kilometres thick. The oceanic crust is the thinnest part, and is only about 8 kilometres thick. Even so, the oceanic crust covers a much wider area.

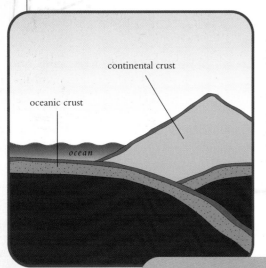

continental crust

oceanic crust

ocean

Rocks of the crust

Many different kinds of rocks are found in both the continental crust and the oceanic crust. Granite is a light-coloured rock that is common in all the continents. A darker, heavier rock called basalt is the main kind in the oceanic crust. Both granite and basalt are formed from different kinds of molten rock that have cooled and hardened.

The Earth's crust has two parts: the continental crust and the oceanic crust.

Although some continents are completely surrounded by water, they are not considered islands. Real islands are smaller than continents. This is even the case for very large islands, such as Greenland, Papua New Guinea and Madagascar. Even though Australia is the world's smallest continent, it is still nearly four times the size of Greenland, the world's largest island.

Shields

Few areas of the ocean floor are more than 150 million years old. On the other hand, several large areas of the continental crust are far more ancient, with rocks up to three and a half billion years old – the oldest rocks on the Earth's surface. These ancient regions are called shields, such as the vast Canadian Shield of North America. A shield is the **exposed** core of a continent, showing lots of rocks like granite. Shields can contain great wealth in minerals like gold, silver, copper and iron ore.

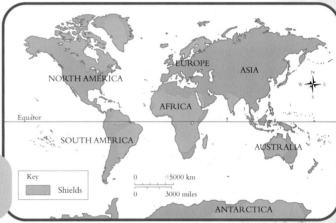

This map shows where the main continental shield areas are located.

Granite is a typical rock of the continents.

CONTINENTAL DRIFT

Up until the mid-1900s, most **geologists** believed that the continents have been fixed in one position since the Earth's beginning. After all, they argued, continents are part of the Earth's crust, which is made entirely of rock. How could continents move, even slowly, when they are embedded in solid rock?

Lystrosaurus

The idea of fixed continents seemed to make sense. Even so, there were some problems. Among them was the *Lystrosaurus* puzzle. *Lystrosaurus* was a hippopotamus-like reptile that lived about 250 million years ago. Its fossil remains have been found on some of the different southern continents, like Africa and Antarctica. But *Lystrosaurus* was a land animal. It could not swim in the sea like a seal or a dolphin. So how could this reptile have spread itself to such distant, unconnected continents, across thousands of kilometres of ocean? The same question had to be asked for several different kinds of prehistoric plants and animals.

Lystrosaurus and its relatives lived in prehistoric Africa, India and Antarctica.

Wegener's theory

In 1912, a German scientist named Alfred Wegener (pronounced *Vay-guh-ner*) came up with a radical idea: that continents move along the surface of the Earth. This idea became known as the **theory** of continental drift. According to this theory, fossil animals, like *Lystrosaurus*, could spread throughout the southern continents because these **landmasses** were joined together 250 million years ago. This theory also explained why certain areas of different continents appear to fit each other like the pieces of a jigsaw puzzle – especially the eastern coast of South America and the western coast of Africa.

Rejection

The theory of continental drift was not popular in Wegener's time. Continental drift may have explained why prehistoric plants and animals could spread so far, but it provided little evidence that continents could actually move. Most geologists continued to believe that the continents stood still and they mocked the theory of continental drift. Any geologist who supported the theory was ridiculed – or even dismissed.

New evidence

By the 1960s, scientific evidence began to support the idea of moving continents. Some of the most important evidence came from new discoveries about the ocean floor. These discoveries changed forever the idea that the continents – or any part of the Earth's crust – do not move.

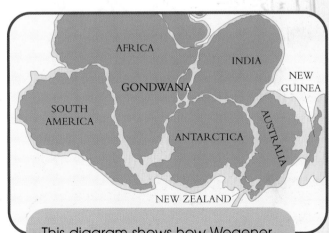

This diagram shows how Wegener thought the southern continents fitted together hundreds of millions of years ago, before drifting apart.

Plate
TECTONICS

During the 1950s and 1960s, scientists made important new discoveries about the Earth. They studied a long ridge beneath the Atlantic Ocean and found that this was an area where the Earth's crust was splitting apart and widening the ocean. They studied the **magnetic properties** of rocks around this area and found that the ocean had been widening for many millions of years. By the 1970s, most scientists no longer believed that the continents lay in fixed, unchanging positions.

Rigid plates

The new **theory** supported the idea of continental drift. But it was a bit different from Wegener's original theory, and explained a lot more about how the continents move. According to the new theory, the Earth's outermost rocky layers are divided up into about 30 huge sections, of different widths and shapes. These sections are rigid and are known as plates or **tectonic** plates. The plates are much bigger than the continents because they include parts of the ocean floor. The new theory became known as plate tectonics ('tectonics' relates to the structure and changes in the Earth's crust).

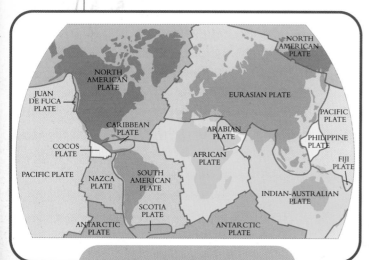

The Earth's tectonic plates include both oceanic crust and continental crust.

Slowly moving

Tectonic plates are made up of rock from the crust and the upper **mantle**. Each plate is about 100 kilometres thick. The rigid plates float on the layer of rocks below, moving sideways along the hot lower surface. When the plates move, anything attached to them moves as well, including continents and parts of the ocean floor. The movement is extremely slow – about 10 centimetres every year (scientists have actually measured this rate). But the plates can cover great distances over millions of years.

The Earth's plates have great variation in area. Most of them include both ocean floor and continental landscapes. The massive Pacific Plate covers most of the Pacific Ocean floor, bordering on regions as far apart as New Zealand and western North America. The Caribbean Plate seems tiny in comparison. It covers a much more compact area of ocean floor and a small area of **Central America** and South America.

Journey of the continents

Scientists believe that about 250 million years ago, the continents of the world all moved together into one giant supercontinent called Pangaea (pronounced *pan-jee-uh*). By 200 million years ago, moving plates below Pangaea had split it into two smaller supercontinents. The northern one – called Laurasia – was made up of Europe, Asia and North America. The southern supercontinent – Gondwana – was made up of South America, Africa, Australia, Antarctica and India (India was a separate **landmass** in ancient times). Laurasia and Gondwana began breaking up about 150 million years ago. Europe and Asia remained close to each other. Africa and India drifted away from the other Gondwana continents and connected with the Asian landmass. South America drifted in a different direction, connecting with North America to form the Americas. Australia and Antarctica became 'island continents' isolated from the other landmasses.

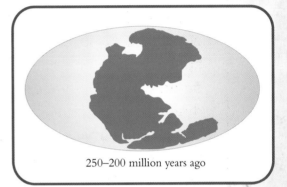

250–200 million years ago

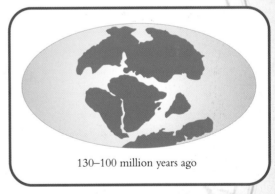

130–100 million years ago

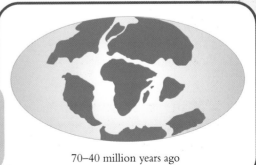

70–40 million years ago

The continents that once belonged to Pangaea are now in very different positions.

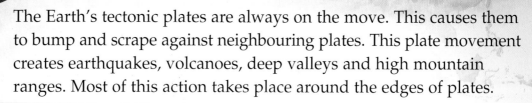

The Earth's tectonic plates are always on the move. This causes them to bump and scrape against neighbouring plates. This plate movement creates earthquakes, volcanoes, deep valleys and high mountain ranges. Most of this action takes place around the edges of plates.

Moving apart

Sometimes the edges of two plates move apart from each other. This results in a great fracture or rift in the Earth. A rift is often accompanied by volcanoes and lava flows, as **molten rock** is pushed up from deep below the crust. Where two plate edges move apart under the ocean, it causes the ocean floor to spread out and widen. Where two plate edges move apart on land, it creates a deep valley. If the valley widens enough, it may become flooded with lakes or sea water. The Great Rift Valley of East Africa is an example of two plate edges moving apart on land. Scientists believe that the Great Rift Valley will continue to widen over millions of years, eventually splitting Africa into two separate **landmasses**.

The Great Rift Valley in East Africa is located where two tectonic plates are moving apart.

Bumping together

Sometimes the edges of two plates bump into each other. When the pressure of the collision becomes great enough, one plate plunges below the other plate. This can result in violent earthquakes, lava eruptions or changes in the crust. If a plate on the ocean floor bumps into the plate of a continent, it creates deep undersea trenches and chains of volcanoes near the coast. If two continental plates bump into each other, the landscape crumples and folds into a great mountain range. The high mountains of the Himalayas were uplifted millions of years ago when the continent of Asia collided with the ancient Indian landmass (because of this collision, India now is part of the Asian continent). Other mountain ranges have been lifted in this way. Hundreds of millions of years before the Himalayas, the Appalachian Mountains were lifted up when North America collided with the Eurasian and African landmasses to form Pangaea.

Moving sideways

Sometimes two plates move sideways along each other's edges. This creates a break in the plates called a fault. The San Andreas Fault in California (between the Pacific Plate and the North American Plate) is a well-known example. Plate edges do not move smoothly and steadily along faults, but in sudden jolts – and each jolt causes an earthquake. Many devastating earthquakes take place along fault zones. The San Andreas Fault causes many earthquakes in California.

Hot spots

Some areas below the crust are extremely hot, with great columns of molten rock pushing upward. These are known as hot spots. Where part of a plate moves over a hot spot, volcanoes can erupt through the plate. As the plate keeps moving, the eruption may continue, but in a different part of the plate. This is why hot spots form chains of volcanoes, such as the volcanic Hawaiian Islands.

Many devastating earthquakes take place along the San Andreas Fault in California.

MOUNTAINS

All continents have mountains and mountain ranges. Most of these mountains were caused by the collision of tectonic plates. Plate collisions may cause volcanic eruptions, or push or fold the rocky layers of continents into peaks and valleys. Mountain ranges are often positioned near the edge of continents. The Andes Mountains follow the coastline of South America and the Atlas Mountains are on the north-eastern edge of Africa. They may also be in the place where two ancient **landmasses** were pushed together, such as the Himalayas (which join India with the rest of Asia) or the Ural Mountains (which join Europe with Asia).

The age of mountains

The shape and size of mountains often depend on their age. Some continents have high ranges with sharp, jagged peaks, like the Alpine Mountains of Europe or the Rocky Mountains of North America. These ranges can be less than 60 million years old, which is young for mountains. Continents also have lower, more worn-down ranges, which can be hundreds of millions of years old. Some of these ranges are so old that they seem more like hills than mountains. The Flinders and Macdonnell ranges of Australia are examples of very ancient mountains.

Older mountains, such as the Purnululu (Bungle Bungle) Range of Australia, are often low and rounded.

Mountains and weather

Mountains often shape the weather patterns on a continent. For example, a high mountain range near the coast can trap rain clouds blown in from the sea. This causes much rain to fall on the coastal side of the ranges, but not much on the inland side. One side may have green slopes of farms and forest, while the other side may be dry, with only a few scattered plants. Mountains on the western coast of North America and the eastern coast of Australia cause such an imbalance of rain.

Dividing the rivers

A long mountain range can mark an important boundary line for rivers and the direction they flow in. This kind of range is called a continental divide. Rivers flowing down opposite sides of a continental divide follow opposite directions. For example, rivers that flow down the eastern side of the Rocky Mountains head towards eastern North America and the Atlantic Ocean. Rivers flowing down the western side head towards western North America and the Pacific Ocean. The Great Dividing Range of Australia is another example of a continental divide.

Younger mountains, such as the Grand Tetons of North America, are often high and jagged.

EROSION

Many landscape features on the continents, such as high mountains and wide valleys, seem permanent. But none of them lasts forever. They are always being attacked and worn away by wind, waves, streams and ice. Even moist air or hot and cold temperatures can wear away landscapes. Anything that wears away the land is called erosion. Sometimes erosion takes place very quickly, but mostly it takes place over long periods of time. Millions of years of erosion can wear down even the tallest mountains.

Shaped by erosion

Erosion shapes many features of the landscape. For example, as water and ice wear away a mountain, they slowly carve out peaks, **gorges**, pinnacles and cliffs. Each time the mountain is eroded, a little more rock and soil is loosened and carried down the slopes. Over time, erosion wears the mountain down to a smaller, more rounded shape. Narrow gorges become broad river valleys, surrounded by low hills. Eventually, the mountain landscape becomes a level plain. However, this kind of erosion can be interrupted whenever the action of tectonic plates causes the land to rise up again, creating new mountains. Then the process of erosion starts all over again.

Rivers in high places often cut deep gorges into the landscape.

Rivers

All continents have river erosion. Rivers normally begin in high places, like mountain slopes. They are caused when rain or melting snow form tiny streams. If these streams meet with other tiny streams they run together to form a larger stream, like a river. The river keeps flowing until it reaches the lowest possible point, which is usually the sea. As the river flows down steep slopes, its current becomes very powerful, dragging gravel and boulders along the steep course. The rocks grind against the riverbed, deepening it into narrow, V-shaped gorges. When the river flows into lower and flatter areas, the riverbed becomes wider and the current becomes calmer. Instead of moving heavy rocks, the current carries mainly fine materials like sand and silt. Even so, the river continues to shape the land, creating wide valleys and **flood plains**.

Caves are often created by erosion. Water that seeps underground can dissolve certain rocks, such as limestone. The water slowly eats away at the limestone, making underground pockets, hollows and tunnels. Over time, a great system of caves is created. Tunnels connecting the caves can form many kilometres of passageways. Water flowing through the tunnels can form a river, complete with underground lakes and waterfalls. Many of the world's deepest caves are in Europe, including the Lamprechtsofen Cave of Austria and the Reseau Jean Bernard of France.

When a river meets the sea, it often creates a fan-shaped region called a **delta**, where tonnes of sand, mud and silt are deposited.

Glaciers

Glaciers are masses of flowing ice. They begin in the high, cold slopes of mountains and flow down to lower regions. Glaciers move much more slowly than rivers. Like rivers, they pick up rocks and carry them along. The rocks grind and scrape against the landscape, carving huge U-shaped valleys into the land. They carve away mountainsides, wear down hills and gouge deep hollows into the land. If a glacier reaches the sea, it begins to melt and break into **icebergs**. Today, glaciers are found on all continents except Australia.

Sheets of ice

A very large glacier is called a continental glacier (sometimes called an icesheet or icecap). Continental glaciers spread out, covering thousands of square kilometres of land. They occur in polar regions, such as Greenland and Antarctica. They have also occurred during very cold periods of the Earth's history, such as an **ice age**. For example, vast areas of Canada and Scandinavia were shaped by continental glaciers during the last ice age.

Glaciers begin in the high cold slopes of mountains.

Erosion in deserts

Hot deserts are dry regions, covered mainly by bare rock and sand. Africa, Asia and Australia have the world's largest hot deserts. These regions have little rainfall or ice to produce rivers or glaciers. Yet hot desert landscapes can be heavily eroded. The land surface does not have a thick protective covering of soil or plants. When rain does fall, the water rushes across the bare ground, carrying tonnes of loose rock and sand into **gullies**.

Waves pounding on the shores slowly wear away the land.

Wave erosion is caused by the action of water and wind. Wind starts the waves by blowing over the sea. The waves move towards the land and break upon the shore. The constant pounding of waves begins to erode the shore. Sea cliffs are worn down to rocks and rocks are worn down to sand. Much of this material is picked up by waves and hurled back against the shore, causing further erosion. Wave erosion shapes inlets, cliffs, rock arches and hollows along the coast.

Desert winds

Desert erosion can also be caused by wind. Wind sweeping across the land picks up the dry earth and blows it away in clouds of dust. Heavier sand grains are blown closer to the land, usually no more than a metre above the surface. The sand grains are blown forcefully, scraping and scratching against anything in their path. Sometimes they grind away the sides and lower surfaces of desert rocks, giving them an odd, mushroom-like shape. Desert winds can also blow sand into big piles called dunes. Winds often change the shape and position of dunes. Shifting dunes in desert areas can cause problems by burying roads and towns.

Wind and sand can erode desert rocks, giving them an odd mushroom-like shape.

Oceans and CONTINENTS

The oceans cover more than two-thirds of the Earth's crust. The oceans are very different from the continents. Even the solid ocean floor is different. Rocks of the ocean floor are generally heavier than rocks of the continents. Undersea plains are flatter than land plains and undersea trenches are deeper than land valleys (the Mariana Trench in the Pacific Ocean reaches more than 11 kilometres below sea level – more than six times deeper than the Grand Canyon). Undersea peaks, cliffs and ridges are often more sharp and jagged than those on land, because deep beneath the sea there is no erosion from wind and ice.

Widening and shrinking

Like the continents, the ocean floor is part of the **tectonic** plates. This means that the ocean floor is always moving, just as the continents are always moving. Undersea plates in the Atlantic Ocean are being pushed apart. This causes the ocean floor to spread out and widen. In the Pacific Ocean, undersea plates are being pushed below the plates of the continents. This causes the ocean floor to become narrower.

One ocean

The oceans have moved and changed a great deal over time. About 250 million years ago, scientists believe there was one huge ocean on Earth, which they call Panthalassa. This was also the time when all the continents were pushed together into the supercontinent of Pangaea. When Pangaea began breaking up into different continents, it also broke Panthalassa into different oceans.

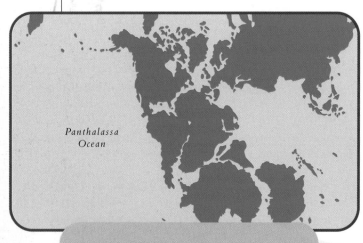

Panthalassa Ocean

250 million years ago, all the oceans of the world formed one great ocean called Panthalassa.

Ancient floods

Sometimes the oceans flood over the continents, forming great inland seas where there once was land. This happened about 100 million years ago in many low-lying areas of Australia, during the **Age of Reptiles**. At other times, the ocean drops back from the continents, forming areas of land where there once was sea. This happened thousands of years ago during the last **ice age**. These changes can be caused by changes in the Earth's climate. If the Earth's climate is warm enough, the polar icecaps melt, causing the sea level to rise throughout the world and flood the continents. Yet if the Earth's climate is cold enough, so much water may turn to ice that the sea level can drop 100 metres and expose more areas of land.

The continental shelf

A continent does not normally end where its land meets the sea. Beyond the shore usually lies a part of the seabed called the continental shelf, which is covered by shallow water and is considered to be part of the continent. In some places, the continental shelf reaches out hundreds of kilometres. Beyond the continental shelf, a sloping surface called the continental slope leads down to the deep ocean floor.

The longest mountain range in the world is below the Atlantic Ocean. This is the Mid-Atlantic Ridge, a winding chain of mountains that stretches for more than 14 000 kilometres in a north–south direction, almost all the way from Iceland to Antarctica. The Mid-Atlantic Ridge has formed where two huge tectonic plates are moving apart, causing volcanic eruptions and the sea floor to spread.

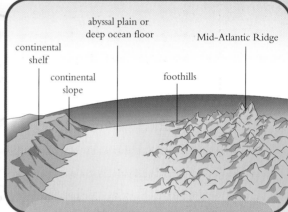

continental shelf

continental slope

abyssal plain or deep ocean floor

foothills

Mid-Atlantic Ridge

The Earth's crust. The continental shelf and continental slope lead down to the deep ocean floor.

This ancient fossil *Diplomystus dentatus* lived in Wyoming, USA, when seas flooded the region millions of years ago.

Climate and
CONTINENTS

Each part of the world has its own pattern of weather throughout the year. This yearly weather pattern is known as climate. The climate of a place can determine what the land looks like, what kinds of plants and animals live there, the way people live and whether there are many people or hardly any at all. The continents are so large that most of them have more than one kind of climate.

Sunshine

Most differences in climate are caused by varying amounts of heat and light received from the Sun. The tropics, a wide zone near the **equator**, receives the most sunshine. Tropical regions (most of South America and Africa) are mainly hot or warm throughout the year. This is very different from the polar zones at the North and South poles, which receive the least sunshine. Polar regions (Antarctica and Greenland) are always cold. Between the equator and the poles lie two large areas called temperate zones. These are zones where the sunshine changes with the seasons. Temperate regions (like most of Europe and North America) have hot, sunny summers and cold, darker winters.

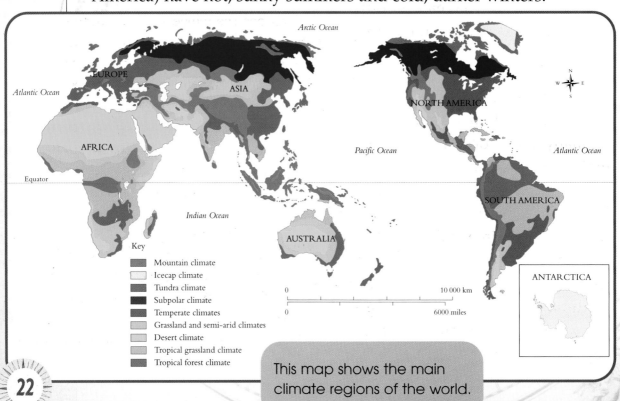

Key

- Mountain climate
- Icecap climate
- Tundra climate
- Subpolar climate
- Temperate climates
- Grassland and semi-arid climates
- Desert climate
- Tropical grassland climate
- Tropical forest climate

This map shows the main climate regions of the world.

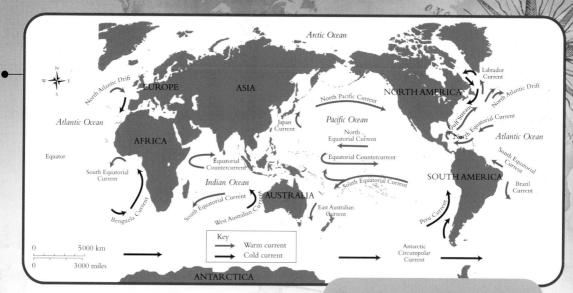

This map shows the world's oceans and their currents in relation to the continents.

Mountain climates

The climates of different regions on the continents do not always fit neatly into tropical, temperate or polar zones. High areas, such as mountains, always have a colder climate than the land below because the air temperature drops as the **altitude** increases. Many tropical mountain areas of South America are high enough to have a temperate or polar climate – even though they lie in the tropical zone.

Wet and dry

Differences in rainfall can also cause differences in climate. Rainfall depends on many conditions, including the moisture of winds and the temperature of sea currents. Polar regions are normally very dry throughout the year (they are sometimes called cold deserts). But rainfall can vary a great deal in tropical and temperate regions. High rainfall can support thick green forests, while lower rainfall can only support grass or scrub. If the rainfall is very low, the result is a desert climate.

Currents and climate

Ocean currents are streams of water that flow in a regular course through the sea. Some ocean currents carry warm water from the tropics into cooler regions, while others carry cold water from the polar regions into warmer regions. The temperature of currents can influence the climate on any land nearby. A warm current, like one along Europe's Atlantic coast, can bring mild winter weather to coastal areas, even when areas further inland are freezing. A cold current, like one along the west coast of South America, can bring cool summer fogs to coastal areas, even when areas further inland are hot. A cold current, like the current flowing along the south-west coast of Africa, brings mainly dry weather. A warm current, like the current flowing along the east coast of Australia, brings much rainfall.

The wildlife of
CONTINENTS

All continents are well known for their special varieties of plants and animals. For example, South America is famous for its rainforests and colourful birds; Asia for its bamboo forests, komodo dragons and pandas; and Africa for its enormous grasslands, with elephants, rhinoceroses, giraffes and ostriches.

Sharing wildlife

Some continents share many of the same kinds of plants and animals. North America, Europe and Asia all have large forest regions of **conifers** and **deciduous trees**. Animals such as bears, wolves, lynxes, foxes and deer live in these forests. North of these forests, in the cold arctic regions, there are animals such as polar bears, arctic foxes, reindeer and seals. North America, Europe and Asia share so much wildlife because they are close together, and this makes it easier for plants and animals to move between them. More than 200 million years ago, when all the continents were pushed closer together, most of them shared similar kinds of prehistoric plants and animals. Since then, the continents have separated, and this kind of sharing has been less common. However, Europe is still joined to Asia, and North America was connected to Asia by a land bridge across the Bering Strait more than 10 000 years ago.

Horses first appeared in prehistoric North America. From there they crossed ancient land bridges, spreading out over Europe and Asia.

Ocean barriers

Some continents have many plants and animals that are found nowhere else in the world. For example, Australia is the only continent with kangaroos, bandicoots, emus, echidnas and platypuses. This is because Australia is an 'island continent', completely surrounded by sea. The sea acts as a barrier, stopping most animals (especially those that cannot swim or fly) from leaving or entering Australia.

Land and climate barriers

High mountains, hot deserts and differences in climate can also act as wildlife barriers. Such barriers sometimes stand between plants and animals on the same continent. The Himalayas act as a barrier separating the wildlife of north and central Asia from the wildlife of tropical south Asia. In a similar way, the vast Sahara Desert acts as a barrier between the wildlife of north Africa and the wildlife of southern Africa. Most plants and animals cannot tolerate the harsh conditions of these barriers, and cannot travel across them.

Wildlife facts

- Tropical regions of the world have the greatest varieties of plants and animals; polar regions have the fewest.
- Africa has the largest land animals.
- South America has the most kinds of birds.
- North America has the tallest and oldest trees.
- Australia has the most marsupials (pouched mammals, such as kangaroos, wombats, possums and bandicoots) and the only monotremes (egg-laying mammals – platypuses and echidnas).
- Europe and Asia have the greatest number of domesticated animals (including horses, cattle, sheep, goats, pigs and reindeer).
- Antarctica has the fewest plants and animals living on land.

Lungfish are found in the southern continents of Australia, Africa and South America. They are fish that can absorb oxygen with either gills or lungs.

People and CONTINENTS

The first people came from the continent of Africa. They crossed into Asia and Europe around one million years ago. (The first known civilisations began in Asia, around 5000–10 000 years ago.) Early people used the gigantic Asian continent as a path to enter North America, South America and Australia. They settled almost every part of these continents, including most of the nearby islands. They did not allow natural barriers, like seas, mountains and deserts to act as permanent barriers. Antarctica is the only continent not permanently settled today.

Populations

Human populations are not distributed equally around the continents – not even on the same continent. Most people live around a continent's rivers or lakes, or on its coasts or **fertile plains**. These are places where fishing, farming, trade and transport are easiest. People are far less numerous in mountain, desert or polar areas.

Of all the continents, Asia has the most people, with the most heavily populated countries (China and India). Africa and Europe also have large populations. Antarctica has the lowest population, with only temporary residents, such as scientists and tourists.

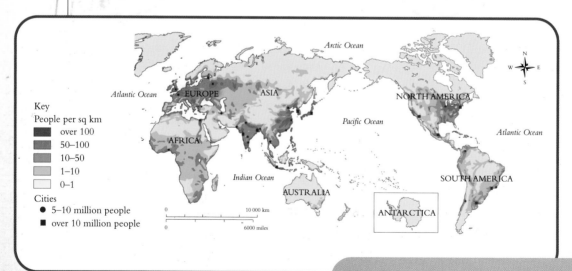

This map shows the density of human populations over the continents.

Cultures

As we have seen, plants and animals of neighbouring continents share many similarities, while the plants and animals of distant continents can be very different. This is often the case for people and their cultures as well – but not always.

Immigration and re-settlement over the past few centuries has mixed up the places where different cultural groups live. For example, Australia lies very close to the Asian country of Indonesia, but these two places have very different cultures. Most Australians and Indonesians have little in common in language, diet, religion or family customs. Yet Australians are very similar in culture to Europeans and North Americans, who live thousands of kilometres away.

Resources

People living on continents take advantage of **natural resources**. These include plants, animals, soil, water, **timber** and minerals. Continents such as North America and Europe are rich in most of these natural resources. Yet huge areas of Africa, Asia and Australia are poor in water or fertile soil. Sometimes natural resources are used up quickly, such as animals that are wiped out through too much hunting, or forests that are wiped out through too much land clearing. People on most continents are taking steps to conserve and protect their natural resources, such as planting more trees, recycling and using what they have more wisely.

European ways

When it comes to culture, Europe has had the biggest influence among the continents. From the 1500s to the 1800s, Europeans conquered and **colonised** most of the continents around the world, especially North America, South America, Africa and Australia. These continents now belong to **independent** countries, no longer ruled by European governments. Even so, many people in these continents still speak a European language or eat and dress in a European manner. Languages such as English, French and Spanish are among the most widespread languages in the world.

The remains of the Temple of Angkor Wat, Cambodia, which was constructed in the 1300s.

27

Relationships between the
CONTINENTS

There are important relationships between the different continents, especially for those that lie close together. There are often similarities in the landscape, climate, wildlife and peoples of neighbouring continents. For people, similarities can result in lasting friendships, associations and **treaties**. There can also be big differences between the people of neighbouring continents, and these can result in disagreement, hostilities and war.

The Old World

Geographers often group the continents according to their relationships. There are several ways this can be done. For example, Europe, Asia and Africa are often grouped together. This makes sense, because the three continents are physically connected. But they have another relationship as well – some of the oldest events in human history took place in Europe, Asia and Africa. This is why these continents are sometimes called 'Old World' continents. Some geographers also include Australia as one of the Old World continents.

The New World

North America and South America are also grouped together as the Americas. They were settled in ancient times by Native Americans (or American Indians), who made their homes in almost every part of these two continents. European civilisation came to the Americas more recently, along with modern cities and countries. For this reason, North America and South America are often called 'New World' continents.

This map shows some of the ways the different continents can be grouped.

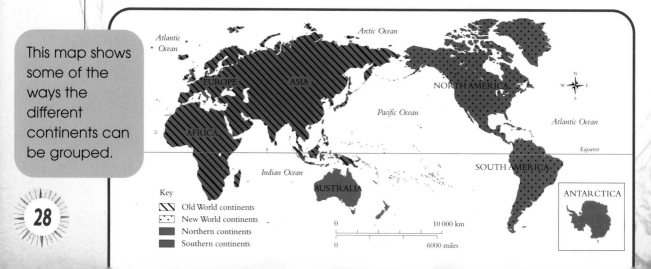

Key
- ⊠ Old World continents
- ⋅ New World continents
- ▨ Northern continents
- ▨ Southern continents

0   10 000 km
0   6000 miles

28

Island continents

Australia and Antarctica are completely surrounded by water and thus isolated from the other continents. Such continents are sometimes called 'island continents'.

North and south

Another way of grouping the continents is by their north–south position. Continents that lie mainly in the **Northern Hemisphere** – Europe, Asia and North America – are sometimes grouped together as the northern continents. Continents that lie more in the **Southern Hemisphere** – Africa, South America, Australia and Antarctica – are sometimes grouped together as the southern continents.

Future changes

Plate tectonics will cause further changes to the continents. Twenty million years from now, scientists believe that East Africa will separate from the rest of the continent, along the Great Rift Valley, and a sea will be created between these landmasses. Some time later, Antarctica will begin to drift slowly north. One hundred and eighty million years later, the East African landmass will collide with Asia, and Antarctica will lie on the tropical equator.

The future

We know that the relationships of continents will change over time. Plate **tectonics** will slowly continue to move these great **landmasses**, and cause great earthquakes and volcanic eruptions. Even with these future dangers, a lot can be done to make the continents safe to live in. Wildlife can be protected from too much hunting and fishing. Land can be protected from **deforestation** and pollution. **Natural resources** can be protected from overuse and waste. And peaceful relations can be promoted between the many different countries.

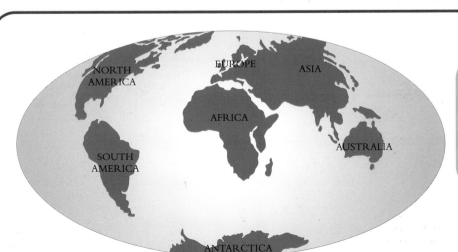

This map shows the possible position of the continents 20–50 million years from today.

GLOSSARY

Age of Reptiles   a time in Earth's history when reptiles became the largest animals (about 250–65 million years ago)

altitude   the height of something, especially above sea level

Central America   the narrow region of North America that lies south of Mexico

colonised   settled in a region; controlling the land and its people

conifers   non-flowering trees or shrubs that bear cones. The leaves can have a needle, oval, scale or barbed shape.

core   central part of the Earth, made up of solid and molten rock (more than 3000 kilometres thick)

deciduous trees   trees that shed their leaves during a certain time of the year, such as autumn

deforestation   clearing away of trees or forests

delta   fan-shaped area formed at the mouth of a river, where the river divides into branches before entering the sea

equator   imaginary line around the middle of the Earth's surface

exposed   laid open to sun, wind and rain

fertile plains   plains that are rich in nutrients and suitable for growing crops and raising livestock

flood plains   plains made up of soil deposited when a river floods

geographers   people who study geography, the study of the Earth's surface

geologists   people who study geology, the study of the Earth

gorges   deep, narrow valleys with steep walls

gullies   narrow channels formed by running water or heavy rains

ice age   a time when parts of the Earth became colder and were covered by glaciers. There have been many ice ages in ancient history.

icebergs   masses of floating ice

independent   not controlled or supported by others

landmasses   large areas of land, such as continents

magnetic properties   characteristics of a magnet

mantle   layer of very dense rock (about 2900 kilometres thick) below the Earth's crust

molten rock rock that has turned to liquid by heat

natural resources supplies of useful materials from nature, such as soil, water or minerals

Northern Hemisphere northern half of the Earth between the North Pole and the equator

Southern Hemisphere southern half of the Earth between the South Pole and the equator

tectonic relating to the structure and changes in the Earth's crust

theory idea, or collection of ideas, put forward to explain certain phenomena or observable events

timber trees or forested land; wood useful for constructing buildings, furniture and wooden objects

treaties recognised agreements, often between nations (such as an agreement to end war or share resources)

FURTHER INFORMATION

Websites

About Geography **geography.about.com**

Includes sites for world atlas and maps, glossary, quizzes and homework help.

National Geographic **www.nationalgeographic.com**

Includes sites for travel, maps, news, nature, history and culture.

Thinkquest: Puzzles of the Earth **http://library.thinkquest.org**

A site all about plate tectonics.

Books

Doherty, G., Claybourne, A. & Davidson, S. *The Usborne-Internet-Linked Encyclopedia of World Geography*. Usborne Publishing Ltd, London, 2001.

Lands and Peoples. Grolier Incorporated, Danbury, 1995.

Parker, S., Morgan, S. & Steele, P. *Collins Ultimate Atlas of Almost Everything*. Harper Collins Children's Books, London, 1998.

Sattler, H. & Maestro, G. *Our Patchwork Planet*. Lothrop, Lee & Shepard Books, New York, 1995.

INDEX